smoothies
and other
blended drinks

smoothies
and other
blended drinks

elsa petersen-schepelern

photography by james merrell

RYLAND
PETERS
& SMALL

LONDON NEW YORK

Art Director	**Jacqui Small**
Art Editor	**Penny Stock**
Editor	**Elsa Petersen-Schepelern**
Production	**Meryl Silbert, Kate MacKillop**
Food Stylist	**Bridget Sargeson**
Stylist	**Ben Kendrick**

Acknowledgments

My thanks to Norah Meany, Jenny Merrell, Peter Bray, Clare Gordon-Smith, Tessa Kerwood, Louise Sherwin-Stark, and Jack Sargeson.

Notes

Take care—not all blenders or food processors are designed to crush ice. If yours isn't, crush the ice separately and spoon into the serving glass before adding the smoothie mixture.
The ice cream scoop measurements used in this book are medium, unless otherwise specified.

First published in the USA in 1997
This paperback edition published in 2004 by
Ryland Peters & Small, Inc.
519 Broadway, 5th Floor
New York, NY 10012
www.rylandpeters.com

10 9 8 7 6 5 4 3 2 1

Text © Elsa Petersen-Schepelern 1997, 2004
Design and photographs © Ryland Peters & Small 1997, 2004

Library of Congress Cataloging-in-Publication Data

Petersen-Schepelern, Elsa.
  Smoothies and other blended drinks / Elsa Petersen-Schepelern ; photography by James Merrell.– 1st American pbk. ed.
    p. cm.
Includes index.
  ISBN 1-84172-635-4
  1. Blenders (Cookery) 2. Smoothies (Beverages) I. Title.
  TX840.B5P4822 2004
  641 .8'75--dc22
                    2003015205

Printed in China

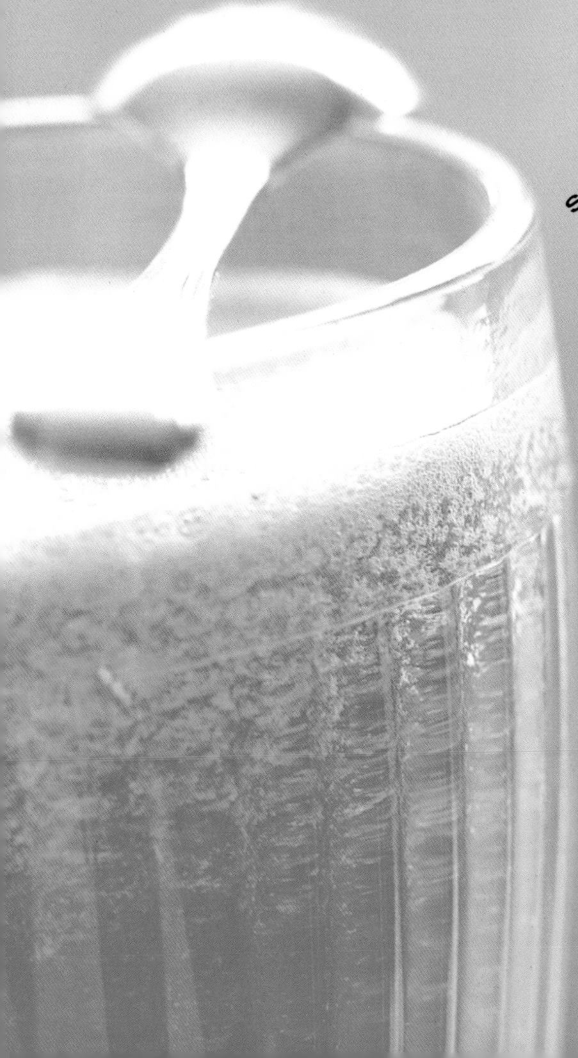

smoothies
and other blended drinks

Blenders, food processors, and juicers have made life much easier and more exciting for us all. Many different kinds of drinks are quickly assembled using any of these wonder machines. A blender, especially one that is strong enough to crush ice, can be used to mix smoothies, milkshakes, lassi yogurt drinks, and cocktails.

The drinks in this book are quickly made in any of these machines, and are based on the ingredients shown here; ice cream, milk, yogurt, ice, fruit, sugar—as well as wine, spirits, and liqueurs.

If you're watching your weight, you can use low-fat milk and yogurt, as well as fresh fruit juice. Many are so delicious you won't even want to add any sugar at all.

If you're a chili fiend—there's good news! Serve one of the yogurt-based drinks— since capsaicin, the chemical in chilies that makes them hot, is fat soluble rather than water soluble, they'll quell the fires a little and allow you to keep munching!

chocolate mocha milkshake

Coffee and chocolate produces the classic mocha mixture. Make this smoothie stronger or sweeter to taste—heaven for chocoholics!

½ **cup espresso coffee, chilled**

4 oz. semisweet chocolate,

or 2 tablespoons chocolate syrup

3-4 scoops vanilla ice cream

½ **cup cold milk, or to taste**

sugar, to taste

to serve

whipped cream

chocolate curls

Purée the coffee and chocolate together in a blender. Add the ice cream and blend again. Add just enough milk to produce the desired consistency, pulse a few times, and add sugar as needed.

Serve topped with a swirl of whipped cream and a sprinkle of chocolate curls.

Serves 1-2

ice cream

smoothies

passionfruit
milkshake with grand marnier

Passionfruit with Grand Marnier or Italian Galliano liqueur is a terrific combination. If you like your milkshake even thicker, add extra ice cream: if you like it smoother, add more milk, to taste.

3 passionfruit, chilled

1 tablespoon Grand Marnier or

Italian Galliano liqueur

3 scoops ice cream

½ cup milk, or to taste

sugar, to taste

Scoop the pulp and seeds of 2 passionfruit into the blender, add the Grand Marnier or Galliano, the ice cream, and milk, then blend. Taste, then add sugar and a little extra milk if preferred. Spoon the remaining passionfruit over the top, then serve.

Serves 1–2

11

A Vienna-coffee-style smoothie—add extra milk if you prefer your coffee creamier, or extra ice cream if you like to stand your spoon up in your coffee!

½ cup espresso coffee, chilled

1 tablespoon Drambuie (optional)

2 scoops vanilla ice cream

½ cup milk, or to taste

sugar, to taste

Place the coffee in a food processor or blender, with the Drambuie, if using. Add the ice cream and half the milk, then blend. Add sugar to taste, and add extra milk if you like your smoothie smoother.

Serves 1–2

coffee ice cream smoothie

ginger shake

If you're a ginger fan, this recipe will be your idea of heaven. Another treat for ginger fiends is what is called a "Ginger Spider" in my native Australia. Place a scoop of ice cream in a soda glass and top with ginger ale. Why a spider? I don't know—but I do know I'm terrified of them!

6 pieces of stem ginger, in syrup

½ cup milk, or to taste

3 scoops ice cream

extra sugar, to taste

to serve (optional)

small scoops of ice cream

extra ginger, chopped

Place the ginger pieces, ice cream, milk, and 6 tablespoons of the syrup in a blender, then purée to a froth. Taste and add extra milk and sugar if preferred. Serve, decorated to taste with another small scoop of ice cream or some extra ginger, chopped.

Serves 1–2

strawberry liqueur smoothie

Old-time American soda jerks were experts, balancing a scoop of ice cream on the edge of the soda glass. If you're not, you could always balance yours on a teaspoon! Make endless variations of this recipe, matching the liqueur to the fruit—Eau de Fraises with strawberries, Poire William with pears, Cassis with blackcurrants, peach liqueur with peaches, or Framboise with raspberries.

A variation on this recipe doesn't even need a blender—make a Strawberry Spider in a tall glass with a scoop of strawberry ice cream, 1 tablespoon of liqueur or strawberry syrup, then top up with soda (preferably strawberry). Pour in the soda very carefully— it will fizz like mad!

8 oz. strawberries

1 tablespoon liqueur, such as Eau de Fraises, Cointreau, or Grand Marnier

3 scoops strawberry ice cream

½ cup milk, or to taste

1 small scoop strawberry ice cream, to serve

Place the first 4 ingredients in a blender and process to a froth. Add extra ice cream for a thicker smoothie, or extra milk, to taste. Serve with a small scoop of ice cream balanced on the edge of the glass.

Serves 1–2

a summer shake with the bright,

sweet scent of ripe berries

passionfruit meringue smoothie

A recipe based on the Pavlova—the national dessert of Australia and New Zealand. It was named in honor of the great Russian ballerina who toured Down Under in the 1920s, when traveling to such frontier territories required a good deal of fortitude.

The Pavlova consists of a large meringue, topped with fresh fruit and whipped cream, then cut into slices like a cake. Passionfruit is almost always included as one of the fruits, plus strawberries in the cooler south of the country and fruits like papaya, mango, and pineapple in the tropical north.

It can be changed according to which fruits are in season and is a particular treat for someone with a sweet tooth. Apply the same seasonal rules to this amazing drink and enjoy yourself!

Make the meringues yourself if you like—but it is much simpler to buy them.

2 small white meringues, about

2 inches in diameter

8 oz. strawberries (or other fruit in season)

2 passionfruit

3 scoops ice cream, or to taste

½ cup milk, or to taste

to serve (optional)

1 tablespoon whipped cream

pulp and seeds of 1 passionfruit

1 meringue, crumbled

Process the meringues, strawberries, and milk in a blender or food processor.

Add the ice cream and the seeds and pulp of 2 passionfruit. Blend again. Taste and add extra milk if you like a thinner drink, or extra ice cream if you like it thicker.

Pour into tall glasses, and serve, topped with the crumbled meringue, passionfruit pulp, and whipped cream, if using.

Serves 1–2

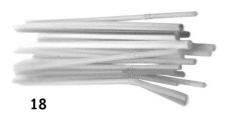

peach melba
shake

Another recipe with connections with Down Under. Peach Melba is another of the world's great desserts, created by legendary French chef Escoffier in honor of the 19th century Australian soprano, Dame Nellie Melba—who must have been something of a gourmet, judging by the number of famous dishes named after her. This liquid variation is wonderful at any time of day.

2 poached peaches (canned or homemade)

2 oz. fresh raspberries

3 scoops vanilla ice cream

½ cup milk, or to taste

to serve (optional)

1 tablespoon crushed flaked almonds

1 tablespoon fresh raspberries

whipped cream

If poaching fresh peaches, place them in a saucepan, add 1 tablespoon of sugar per peach, and cover with water or white wine. Bring to a boil and simmer for about 6 to 10 minutes until tender. Cool, slip off the skins, then remove the pits and chill the fruit. Keep the syrup to sweeten the shake.

Place the fruit, ice cream, and milk in a blender or food processor and blend until foaming. Add extra ice cream or extra milk, to taste. Serve, sprinkled with crushed almonds, raspberries, or whipped cream.

Serves 1–2

Overleaf: Peach Melba shake (left) and Passionfruit meringue smoothie (right).

A slimming but filling breakfast—full of flavor, packed with healthy calcium and fiber, and very good for you! If you like your drinks less sweet, reduce the quantity of honey. Other fruit in season, such as berries, can also be substituted. Use chilled fruit to make smoothies—but never put bananas in the refrigerator—or anywhere near citrus fruit— they don't like it. They quickly turn black in the refrigerator, and become over-ripe in a flash if introduced to a citrus fruit.

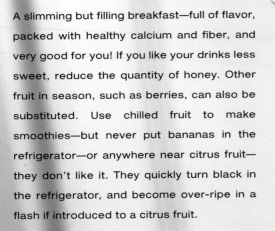

banana and honey
breakfast smoothie

1 cup low-fat milk

1 cup plain low-fat yogurt

½ cup crushed ice

1 tablespoon honey

1 banana

1 tablespoon wheat germ

Place all the ingredients in the blender and process. Add extra fruit if preferred.

Serves 2-4

yogurt drinks

Lassis are a traditional yogurt drink in India, served plain, sweet, or salty—perfect coolers in hot weather. This is a very indulgent form of lassi—but you can take refuge in the fact that yogurt and ginger are very calming for upset stomachs. Use low-fat yogurt if you prefer, and substitute almost any fruit you have on hand, including non-tropical ones like pears, apricots, or peaches. If you use ginger a lot, it's worth making a quantity of purée and keeping it in the refrigerator. Soak 8 oz. of fresh root ginger in water overnight, peel, then purée in a food processor with a little water: it will keep for up to a month.

Place all the ingredients in a blender or food processor and blend. Serve, poured over crushed ice and garnished with mint.

Serves 2-3

flavored yogurt

1 cup peeled, seeded papaya

1 cup crushed pineapple

or pineapple juice

1 banana

1 cup plain yogurt

1 tablespoon puréed fresh ginger

juice and grated zest of 1 lime

to serve

crushed ice

sprigs of mint

tropical fruit lassi
with papaya ginger and lime

drinks are **India's** favorite coolers

vanilla or chocolate
yogurt lassi

Yogurt drinks are traditionally served with hot Indian curries, some of which can be amazingly spicy. Capsaicin, the chemical in chilies that makes them hot, is not water-soluble, so drinking water, alcohol, or tea will not cool your mouth. Milk or yogurt are the perfect antidote, so this is a wonderful drink to serve with any dish containing chilies.

In India, lassis are flavored with rosewater, saffron, pistachio nuts, or spices such as cardamom. Vanilla and chocolate flavors are more familiar to Western tastes, but you could also experiment and create your own.

1⅓ cups plain low-fat yogurt

1⅓ cups low-fat milk

1 cup crushed ice (optional)

1 tablespoon sugar, or to taste

a choice of:

2 tablespoons chocolate syrup,

or a few drops of vanilla extract,

or 1 teaspoon each of rosewater and crushed cardamom seeds

Blend the yogurt, milk, and crushed ice in a blender or food processor. Add the chosen flavoring and blend again. Taste and add sugar if preferred.

Serves 1–2

27

Mango, papaya, or banana are perfect fruits to team with milk and yogurt. More unusual is passionfruit and 1 teaspoon Grand Marnier or Galliano liqueur. Milk and yogurt are great sources of calcium—use the low-fat kind if you're watching your waistline.

Yogurt and bananas are good if you have an upset stomach, so you might try this drink as a hangover cure!

The variation below, Savory Yogurt Lassi with Spices, is served as an accompaniment to spicy curry dishes all over India, instead of beer or wine. Salty drinks are very cooling in the searing heat of a true Indian summer!

Variation:

Savory Yogurt Lassi with Spices

Instead of the fruit and sugar listed in the main recipe, substitute 1 teaspoon crushed cumin seeds and salt to taste, then serve.

1 cup plain low-fat yogurt

½ cup low-fat milk

6 large strawberries

choice of fruit, such as:

1 cup raspberries, or

8 oz. apricots or peaches, pitted

sugar, to taste

crushed ice, to serve

Place all the ingredients except the sugar and ice in the blender, and process. Taste, add sugar if preferred, and pour into a glass with crushed ice.

Serves 2-4

fruit salad lassi with strawberries

29

coconut with cloves

To make your own coconut milk, place about 6 tablespoons dried unsweetened coconut in a bowl, and cover with milk or water. Let stand for 20 minutes, then press through a strainer. If you don't want to use coconut milk at all, substitute ordinary milk plus coconut syrup, or any kind of fruit syrup.

½ cup milk

1 cup coconut milk (see above)

3 scoops ice cream

1 teaspoon ground cloves

sugar, to taste

to serve (optional)

crushed ice

finely sliced fresh coconut

Place the milk, coconut milk, ice cream, and cloves in the blender, and process until frothy. Taste and add sugar if required. Blend again until all the sugar has dissolved. Serve poured over crushed ice, topped with finely sliced coconut.

Serves 1–2

asian flavors

pineapple apricot
yogurt smoothie

A recipe with ingredients from opposite ends of India—apricots from the romantic Vale of Kashmir in the shadow of the Himalaya, and pineapples from the tropical south. Use fresh apricots if you like, but I find their sweetness is not to be relied upon.

6 fresh or dried apricots, pitted

1 cup fresh pineapple pieces or

canned unsweetened pineapple

1½ cups plain yogurt

sugar, to taste

to serve

crushed ice

chopped fresh apricot (optional)

If using dried apricots, soak them overnight in cold water to cover.
Blend the pineapple with the apricots and yogurt. Sweeten to taste, then pour over crushed ice.
Serve, topped with chopped apricot, if using.
Serves 2-3

Coconut milk and bananas are a traditional Thai combination—I've added dark rum as an optional extra. The result is a Thailand-meets-the-Caribbean mixture! The mango variation (shown far right, recipe below) can be made with fresh mango, or canned Alphonso mango purée. Usually, I'm not an advocate of using other than fresh produce. However, if you can find canned Alphonso mango in an Asian market, buy it and try it. The Alphonso is famous as the world's greatest mango—and believe me, it is! Indians are connoisseurs of mangoes—they have hundreds of varieties and use them fresh, cooked, juiced, turned into chutneys, cooked green with meat, served as salads, and in countless other ways.

about 1 cup canned coconut milk

1 cup low-fat milk

2 ripe bananas

1 tablespoon dark rum (optional)

sugar, to taste

crushed ice, to serve

Place all the ingredients in the blender except the sugar and ice. Blend, adding sugar and more rum, to taste. Pour over crushed ice and serve.

Serves 1-2

Variation:

Coconut Milk with Mango

Use 1 cup Alphonso mango purée or 1 large, ripe, fresh mango instead of the bananas and rum. Blend until frothy and serve with a scoop of mango ice cream.

coconut banana shake

34

great **tropical** ingredients

give the taste of Thailand

pineapple and
lime rush

Also delicious made with ice cream rather than yogurt or coconut milk. If keeping cut pineapple in the refrigerator, first wrap it in plastic film to prevent tainting. Fruit varies in sweetness, so taste the crush before serving and add sugar if necessary.

1½ cups plain yogurt or coconut milk

1 cup chopped fresh ripe pineapple

juice and grated rind of 2 limes

1 cup crushed ice

sugar, to taste

to serve (optional)

finely sliced fresh coconut

1 scoop vanilla ice cream

Place the first 4 ingredients in a blender and process. Taste and add sugar if needed. Serve, decorated with the fresh coconut or a scoop of ice cream, if preferred.
Serves 1–2

banana honey and soy
milk smoothie

A good breakfast smoothie—full of protein from the soy milk. It is quite sweet, so taste it before you add any extra honey. Other fruits, such as strawberries, bananas, or papaya, can be used instead of the banana.

1 banana

1 teaspoon honey

1 cup soy milk

1 cup crushed ice (optional)

sprigs of mint, to serve (optional)

Place the banana, honey, and soy milk in a blender with the crushed ice, if using, and blend. Serve, topped with sprigs of mint.
Serves 1

orange juice
and strawberry crush

A recipe that can be adapted for any fruit in season—just make sure to chill them all (except the banana). You can process them in a blender, or put them through a juice extractor if you prefer your drink a little smoother. If you use apples, remember to add the orange juice immediately so the apples don't go brown.

1 banana

3 ripe apricots, pitted

6 ripe red strawberries

juice of 1 large orange

3 scoops ice cream

1 cup milk, or to taste

Place all the fruit in the blender with half the milk and blend. Add the ice cream and remaining milk, to taste, and blend again.

Serves 2

sodas and crushes

a perfect summer cooler

zippy with ginger

Indian and Moroccan sharbats are distantly related to the sherbets which are familiar to Westerners. They were introduced by the Moghul emperors who invaded India over its North West Frontier in the 16th century.

If you have a juice extractor, use it to make watermelon juice—though I must admit I prefer the thicker consistency produced by a food processor. You can buy ginger purée in supermarkets, but if you can't find it, just peel fresh ginger root and purée in a food processor with a little water or lemon juice, then freeze in small quantities for future use.

1 small, ripe watermelon, chilled

2 tablespoons ginger purée

(or more, to taste)

water (see method)

sugar, to taste

crushed ice, to serve

watermelon
and ginger
sharbat

Cut the watermelon in wedges, remove and discard the rind and seeds. Blend the flesh in a food processor with the ginger. Add water if the mixture is too thick. Taste and add sugar if needed. Serve over crushed ice.
Serves 2–4

Variation:

Almond Sharbat

Grind 4 oz. skinned almonds in a blender, adding a little water to make a smooth paste. Add a few drops of almond essence (optional), 2 cups water, the crushed seeds from 8 green cardamom pods, 1 teaspoon rosewater (optional) and sugar to taste. Blend, then taste and add more sugar if preferred. Pour over crushed ice and serve.

41

Bananas and limes are typical Southeast Asian ingredients, as is ginger, though not usually in this form. Lychees, if you can find them, make a delicious substitute for the bananas—they are sold either fresh or canned in Asian markets.

2-3 large bananas

grated zest and juice of 2 limes

ginger ale, to taste

crushed ice

sugar, to taste

Purée the bananas in a blender with the lime zest and juice, and a little ginger ale. Taste and add sugar if preferred. Place crushed ice in the bottom of each glass, pour over the mixture, and top up with more ginger ale.
Serves 2

bananas and limes
with ginger ale

pineapple with Jamaican ginger beer

Ginger beer is a favorite drink in Jamaica. Put it together with fresh pineapple, and you have an utterly delicious thirst-quencher—the taste of the Caribbean through a straw! Try it mixed with other fresh fruit too, like very ripe peaches, papayas, or apricots.

3 slices ripe fresh pineapple, chilled

about 1½ cups ginger beer, chilled

about 1 cup crushed ice

Purée the pineapple in a blender with the crushed ice and 2 to 3 tablespoons of ginger beer. Pour into tall glasses and top up with the remaining ginger beer.

Serves 1–2

mint and ginger yogurt soda

Mint and ginger make a gorgeous combination. Ginger purée is sold in some supermarkets—or make it yourself with fresh ginger in a blender. Plain yogurt has a wonderful lemony taste. I must admit I prefer this drink without sugar—so taste it first and decide for yourself.

1½ cups plain low-fat yogurt

leaves from 4 sprigs fresh mint

1-inch piece of root ginger, minced, or 1 tablespoon ginger purée

2 cups soda water, or to taste

sugar, to taste

crushed ice, to serve

Place the yogurt, mint, and ginger in a blender with about ½ cup soda, and blend. Add sugar if preferred. Place crushed ice in the bottom of each glass, pour over the mixture, then top up with soda water.

Serves 2–4

spicy, sweet, and cool—**ginger**,
mint, pineapple, and yogurt

Freshly crushed tomato juice is a far cry from the commercial variety. There are many juicers and crushers available now, but if you don't have one, just blend ripe tomatoes in your food processor or blender, then press through a strainer (hard work, but worth it!) Taste the juice before adding any sugar.

Try this recipe if you grow your own fruit, or at the height of summer, when tomatoes are cheap, ripe, and plentiful.

This method can also be used to produce fresh tomato soup (hot or cold), perhaps with a splash of chicken stock, and sprinkled with torn basil leaves. If serving hot, heat the soup just a little, to keep the fresh tomato flavor. To make homemade tomato paste, reduce the pulp over a gentle heat.

2 lb. ripe red plum tomatoes

lemon juice, to taste

salt and pepper, to taste

sugar (optional)

Tabasco sauce (optional)

crushed ice

to serve

sprigs of mint

lemon zest (optional)

Cut the tomatoes into quarters and pass through a juicer. Add lemon juice to keep the color bright, then salt and pepper to taste. Add sugar and Tabasco sauce, if using. Serve with lots of crushed ice, a sprig of mint, and a sprinkle of lemon zest, if using.

Serves 4

homemade
tomato crush

46

Juicers are wonderful machines. Fresh foaming carrot juice is my favorite—but try this spicy combination too. You could substitute 2 seeded chilies instead of the Tabasco sauce, for a fresh, bright chili taste.

tomato celery and carrot crush

2 lb. carrots, chilled

3 stalks celery, chilled

1 lb. tomatoes, chilled

Tabasco sauce, to taste

salt and freshly ground black pepper

crushed ice, to serve

Push the carrots, celery, and tomatoes through a juicer. Alternatively, blend in a food processor with 1 cup iced water, then press through a strainer. Add salt, pepper, and Tabasco, to taste. Serve over crushed ice.

Serves 4–6

campari ruby
grapefruit
crush

A wonderful drink for a summer brunch party. Serve it as a welcoming drink—one tall glass per person—with a romantic or celebration brunch of toasted briôche with smoked salmon and scrambled eggs garnished with snipped chives. Use ruby grapefruit if you can find them—2 or 3 juicy ones will produce this amount of juice. Serve in a huge glass pitcher so guests can help themselves. Campari isn't very intoxicating, so this is a perfect drink for early in the day—and great as a pre-dinner drink in summer too.

2 cups ruby grapefruit juice, chilled

4 tablespoons Campari, or to taste

crushed ice

sprigs of mint, to serve

Blend 1 cup of crushed ice with the Campari and grapefruit juice. Half-fill a pitcher with more crushed ice, pour in the mixture, cram the top of the jug with mint sprigs and serve. **Serves 2-4**

cocktails
and coffee

Grenadine is a beautiful jewel red and made from pomegranates, but you could also use Cointreau, or fresh pomegranate juice, with its slightly bitter taste. (Easy to make—just cut the fruit in half and squeeze over a lemon-squeezer). This is a serious cocktail—if you'd like less alcohol, reduce the quantity of rum and increase the amount of ice—or dilute it with ginger ale.

½ cup crushed pineapple or pineapple juice

½ cup orange juice

1 cup white rum, or to taste

crushed ice

3 tablespoons Grenadine, Cointreau, or fresh pomegranate juice, to serve

If using fresh pineapple, peel it first, making sure all the "eyes" are removed, then quarter and core. Pass through a juicer, or blend in a food processor (for a chunkier consistency). Process the pineapple juice, orange juice, rum, and ice in a blender. Serve in chilled glasses, drizzled with Grenadine, Cointreau, or pomegranate juice. Serves 2-4

jamaican rum punch

The spicy tastes in the traditional Bloody Mary are usually provided by Tabasco sauce. The Food Editor of *Marie Claire* magazine makes her own chili vodka. You could use this instead of the Tabasco for a drink with a bright, clear taste. Test the vodka after 1 day and remove the chili if it's spicy enough. If not, leave for another couple of hours. Take care, and keep tasting, because you can easily make the vodka too hot!

1 cup tomato juice

1 teaspoon Worcestershire sauce

1 tablespoon lemon juice

1 cup crushed ice

1 lemon wedge

1 celery stalk

chili vodka

1 bottle vodka

2 serrano chilies,

halved and seeded

bloody mary with
chili vodka

To make the chili vokda, place the chilies in the bottle of vodka and leave overnight. Taste, leave longer if preferred, then discard the chilies. Keep the vodka in the refrigerator. To make the Bloody Mary, place the tomato juice in a blender with the Worcestershire sauce, lemon juice, 1 measure of chili vodka and the crushed ice. Blend, then pour into tall glasses and serve with a wedge of lemon and a stalk of celery.

Serves 1

Variation:

Not-very-bloody Mary

Omit the vodka and chilies. Add Tabasco, to taste. Proceed as in the main recipe.

fruit-flavored gin makes a **sophisticated** cocktail

Place the blueberries in a large glass bottle. Add the sugar and gin, shake well, and set aside for at least 2 weeks, or up to 2 months. Shake the bottle from time to time—you will see the marvelous rich color developing as the days go by.

When ready to serve, place a shot of the gin in a blender with ½ cup crushed ice. Blend and pour into long chilled glasses. Add a sprig of mint and tonic to taste.

Alternatively, serve alone in small aquavit-style glasses. Do not drive!

blueberry gin

Sloe gin is one of the great traditional British Christmas-time drinks. Sloes—the fruit of the blackthorn—are gathered in the hedgerows after the first frosts in fall, then placed in bottles with gin and sugar, and set aside until Christmas. I think it should be drunk in small glasses—it tastes wonderful, but is very strong, and can be something of a trap. Blueberry gin is a variation on a theme. Serve it straight in small glasses—or in long ones with ice and tonic water. Delicious and the most marvelous color!

1 cup blueberries

6 tablespoons sugar

1 large bottle (750 ml) gin

to serve (optional)

crushed ice

tonic water

sprigs of mint

coffee frappé

A wonderful pick-me-up on a hot summer afternoon—and one that can be adapted to other ingredients, such as tomato juice, orange and raspberry juice, pear or apricot nectar, crushed pineapple with some extra juice added, and so on.

6 tablespoons freshly ground coffee

4 cups boiling water

sugar, to taste

to serve (optional)

¼ cup whipped cream

2 oz. shaved semisweet chocolate

Put the coffee in a French press coffee pot and add boiling water. Leave for 3 minutes, pour into a pitcher with sugar to taste. It should be sweeter than you would usually like. Cool, then freeze in a shallow plastic tray. When solid but not rock-hard, process in a blender, then pour into cups or glasses. Top with cream and chocolate, or serve plain.

Serves 6

white rum and fresh mango
—a great **tropical** cocktail

Use white rum in this recipe for a pretty, clear summer look. However, I grew up in the tropics and I much prefer dark rum; I would always use it instead. New Zealand food writer Clare Ferguson has come up with a marvelous rum idea—keep 2 vanilla beans in a bottle of rum and use it in drinks and for cooking. It smells like the very best rum and raisin ice cream!

1 large ripe mango
juice of 1 lemon
½ cup white rum
(or dark if preferred)
sugar, for glass
crushed ice

Peel the mango and slice the flesh into a blender. Add the lemon juice, rum, and 1 cup crushed ice, then blend.
Rub the cut lemon around the rim of a glass and press into sugar. Place more crushed ice in the glass and pour over the crush.
Serves 1

mango and rum crush

thick tropical crush

This tropical crush is so thick and wonderful it's almost a soup. It will serve one person as a smoothie, and about six people as a champagne cocktail. Don't forget to chill all the fruits first—but wrap up any aromatic ones in plastic wrap to prevent tainting.

tropical fruits such as:

8 oz. cubed fresh papaya

1 cup cubed fresh pineapple

chilled champagne (see method)

sugar, to taste (optional)

watermelon pieces, to serve

Process the fruits in the blender with ½ cup champagne. Add sugar to taste, if using. Pour into a chilled glass, and serve with the watermelon. Alternatively, divide between 6 glasses, top with champagne, and serve as champagne cocktails.

Serves 1 or 6

62

Index

Conversion Chart

Weights and measures have been rounded up or down slightly to make measuring easier.

volume equivalents:

american	metric	imperial
1 teaspoon	5 ml	
1 tablespoon	15 ml	
¼ cup	60 ml	2 fl.oz.
⅓ cup	75 ml	2½ fl.oz.
½ cup	125 ml	4 fl.oz.
⅔ cup	150 ml	5 fl.oz. (¼ pint)
¾ cup	175 ml	6 fl.oz.
1 cup	250 ml	8 fl.oz.

weight equivalents:

imperial	metric
1 oz.	25 g
2 oz.	50 g
3 oz.	75 g
4 oz.	125 g
5 oz.	150 g
6 oz.	175 g
7 oz.	200 g
8 oz.	250 g
9 oz.	275 g
10 oz.	300 g
11 oz.	325 g
12 oz.	375 g
13 oz.	400 g
14 oz.	425 g
15 oz.	475 g
16 oz.	
(1 lb.)	500 g
2 lb.	1 kg

measurements:

inches	cm
¼ inch	5 mm
½ inch	1 cm
¾ inch	1.5 cm
1 inch	2.5 cm
2 inches	5 cm
3 inches	7 cm
4 inches	10 cm
5 inches	12 cm
6 inches	15 cm
7 inches	18 cm
8 inches	20 cm
9 inches	23 cm
10 inches	25 cm
11 inches	28 cm
12 inches	30 cm

oven temperatures:

225°F	110°C	Gas ¼
250°F	120°C	Gas ½
275°F	140°C	Gas 1
300°F	150°C	Gas 2
325°F	160°C	Gas 3
350°F	180°C	Gas 4
375°F	190°C	Gas 5
400°F	200°C	Gas 6
425°F	220°C	Gas 7
450°F	230°C	Gas 8
475°F	240°C	Gas 9